The Rockwool Foundation Research Unit

Study Paper No. 102

Job Quality by Entrepreneurial Spinoffs

Johan M. Kuhn,
Nikolaj Malchow-Møller and
Anders Sørensen

University Press of Southern Denmark

Odense 2015

Job Quality by Entrepreneurial Spinoffs

Study Paper No. 102

Published by:
The Rockwool Foundation research Unit and
University press of Southern Denmark

Address:
The Rockwool Foundation Research Unit
Soelvgade 10, 2.tv.
DK-1307 Copenhagen K

Telephone	+45 33 34 48 00
E-mail	forskningsenheden@rff.dk
web site:	www.en.rff.dk

ISBN 978-87-93119-29-1
ISSN 0908-3979

November 2015

Job Quality by Entrepreneurial Spinoffs

Johan M. Kuhn, Department of International Economics and Management, Copenhagen Business School, Porcelænshaven 16A, DK-2000 Frederiksberg, Denmark (tel: +45 3815 3467, email: jmk.int@cbs.dk)

Nikolaj Malchow-Møller, Department of Business and Economics, University of Southern Denmark, Campusvej 55, 5230 Odense M, Danmark (tel: +45 6550 2109, email: nmm@sam.sdu.dk)

Anders Sørensen (corresponding author), Department of Economics, Copenhagen Business School, Porcelænshaven 16 Porcelænshaven 16A, DK-2000 Frederiksberg, Denmark (tel: +45 3815 3493, email: as.eco@cbs.dk).

Abstract:

We study whether entrepreneurial spinoffs are important drivers of industry dynamics. More precisely, we investigate whether the quality of jobs in spinoff entrepreneurs are higher than for other entrepreneurs. We distinguish spinoff firms by different types and distinguish between growing and declining industry-region clusters. We find that spinoffs on average have higher wages, are more skill intensive, have higher sales per worker and are more productive than non-spinoff entrepreneurial firms. The differences are more pronounced in growing clusters. The results even hold when we control for worker heterogeneity and industry and region clusters characteristics. An important feature of the analysis is that we measure the entrepreneur as the organic new firm. By organic new firm, we mean new firms that are not the result of restructurings or organising existing or additional activities in a formally new firm.

Keywords: Entrepreneurship, Spinoffs, job quality, productivity

JEL: L1

Acknowledgements: We are grateful to the Rockwool Foundation for funding of this project, and Statistics Denmark for providing the data. Thanks to Jan Rose Skaksen, Søren Leth-Petersen, Mette Ejrnæs, Pernille Bang and Zuzanna Tilewska for helpful comments.

1 Introduction

Corporate spinoffs are important drivers of industry dynamics and their study has become an integral part of industrial organisation economics. Identifying characteristics of successful start-ups is an important task in the understanding of the characterization of spinoffs. Spinoffs, defined in different ways, have in numerous studies been shown to be successful in terms of survival (e.g., Phillips 2002, Agarwal et al. 2004, Dahl and Reichstein 2007), profitability (Dahl and Sorenson, 2014), or innovation (Agarwal et al., 2004). Also, there are a few papers studying spinoffs' employment creation (Roberts et al., 2011, and Fryges et al., 2014); which is of specific interest from a policy perspective.[1] Roberts et al. (2011) find that firms with prior industry experience (from the wine industry) are larger than firms without such experience, whereas Fryges et al. (2014) cannot establish evidence for size differences across different types of spinoffs.

In this paper, we consider the characteristics of jobs in spinoff firms as compared to jobs in non-spinoff entrepreneurial firms; an issue that have not yet been addressed in the literature. If spinoffs are to play an important role as an engine for growth and prosperity, we would expect jobs created by these firms to be of higher quality that jobs created in other entrepreneurial firms. We measure this along a number of dimensions: average wage rate, education intensity, and productivity.

Spinoffs are new firms that are defined on the basis of the founder's employment in the year prior to starting the start-up. If the founder has been employed in the same industry as the start-up in the year prior to starting the firm, the founder is considered to have industry experience and the firm to be a spinoff. We distinguish between two different types of spinoffs: spinoff with more than one person moving from a previous firm to the start-up and spinoff with one person moving only. This incorporates the strength of parent-progeny relationships in worker flows (Eriksson and Kuhn, 2006), which might be assumed to be correlated to determinants like organisational heritage (e.g., Phillips, 2002, Helfat and Lieberman, 2002) such as mutual trust of the founders of the spinoff, and other selection issues.

A very important aspect of the paper is that entrepreneurs are measured as organic new firms. By organic new firm, we mean that the firm is not a result of restructurings or a result of organising

---

[1] The term spinoff is used for many different kinds of startups in the literature, the encompassing idea being that there is a transfer of assets from an origin organization to a start-up. The origin organizations can be public research institutions like universities (e.g., Callan, 2001), technological transfer offices (e.g., Cooper, 1985), or private firms. The transfer of assets can be patents or licenses, business or product ideas (Fryges et al, 2014), industry-specific knowledge, like in the present paper, or just everything that travels when one or more individuals move from an existing organization to a new one.

existing or additional activities in a formally new firm. Thereby, the organic new firm must not have existed previously under a different name, with a different owner, or in another legal form (personally owned, incorporated, etc.). Furthermore, the firm must not have been started by persons who are already registered as business owners. Nor may the new firm be a re-start of a business after closure, or a result of changes in the firm-registration information. In sum, the set of entrepreneurial firms used in this paper is much more likely to reflect organic start-ups than if we had simply used the set of all new establishments or firms, which have been common practice in the literature.

We take the business environment of firms into account in addition to distinguishing organic new firms into spinoffs and non-spinoffs. This is motivated by the fact that a large share of entrepreneurial activity is not pulled by new market opportunities. Push factors like dissatisfaction with or separation from an earlier employment relationship or lack of alternative employment opportunities also play an important role, see, *e.g.*, Amit and Muller (1995). As a consequence, a large share of the jobs created by spinoffs are not created in business environments reflecting new market opportunities, but rather in stable or contracting markets, and this is likely to affect the quality and characteristics of the jobs created. To account for this, we distinguish between firms located in growing industry-region clusters and firms located in declining industry-region clusters. That is, we compare jobs in spinoffs in growing (declining) clusters and jobs in non-spinoff entrepreneurial firms in growing (declining) clusters.

We base our analysis on Danish employer-employee register data that almost cover the entire private sector of the Danish economy. An important aspect of the applied employer-employee dataset is that workers are linked to firms and we are able to determine the worker characteristics such as age, gender and education in firms.

The main results established are that spinoffs on average have higher wages, are more skill intensive, have higher sales per worker and are more productive than other new firms. Especially, we find that spinoffs are more productive than non-spinoff entrepreneurial firms: labour productivity in spinoffs is up to one fourth larger than in non-spinoffs, whereas total factor productivity is up to 12 percent larger than for non-spinoff entrepreneurial firms. The results even hold in the case even when dummies that control for observed and unobserved differences at the cluster level are included in the regressions.

The main contribution of this paper is to investigate the characteristics of jobs in spinoffs compared to jobs in non-spinoff entrepreneurial firms using a measure of the entrepreneur as the organic new firm. It should be emphasised that the purpose of this paper is not to present a causal relationship for job quality and firm types. The study is rather a study of facts for the raw and conditional differences between jobs in spinoffs and other entrepreneurial firms. It is therefore not clear whether the results are biased by for example selection of different types of individuals into different types of firms. We leave this important issue for future research.

The paper is organised as follows. We present the data and basic definitions in section 2. Section 3 presents the empirical approach. In Section 4, we present our results, where we compare spinoffs and non-spinoff entrepreneurial firms. Section 5 concludes.

2 Data and Definitions

We use matched worker-firm data covering almost the entire private sector of the Danish economy for the period 2001-10. The data are drawn from different Danish registers administered by *Statistics Denmark*.

First, the *General Enterprise Statistics* builds on the *Central Business Register* and contains annual information about all active firms in the Danish economy. From this database, we get information about, *e.g.*, industry, region, sales, capital input, intermediate inputs and number of workers of all firms in the private sector.

Second, we use the *Statistics on New Enterprises*, which identifies, for each year between 2001 and 2010, all the new start-ups. This includes both personally-owned and incorporated firms that fulfil a number of conditions that allow us to consider them as being organic new firms in a given year, see the next paragraph for a precise description. We use this database to identify all the start-ups among all the active firms in the *General Enterprise Statistics*.

Note that Statistics Denmark has undertaken extensive efforts to identify the organic new firms. Many of the formally new firms may thus be the results of restructurings or the results of organising existing or additional activities in formally new enterprises. As a consequence, for firms to appear in the *Statistics on New Enterprises*, they must not only be newly registered at the business authorities for VAT-taxation, it is also required that the firms must not have existed previously under a different name, with a different owner, or in another legal form (personally owned, incorporated, etc.).

Furthermore, they must not have been started by persons who are already registered as business owners at the VAT authorities. The data are also cleaned for re-starts of businesses after closure, and changes in the firm-registration information; see Statistics Denmark (2002) for more details. Finally, we have removed an additional 0.2 per cent of observations in the *Statistics on New Enterprises*, where supplementary information in the *General Enterprise Statistics* suggests that the firm was established before 2001. In sum, the set of new firms used in this paper is much more likely to reflect organic start-ups than if we had simply used the set of all new establishments or all new firms, which have been common practice in the literature.

The *Statistics on New Enterprises* is restricted to industries that *Statistics Denmark* categorises as "business-related industries". This excludes the public sector and (most of) the primary sector, as well as industries with activities that are not liable to VAT, such as dentists, transportation of persons, banking *etc.* Furthermore, the *Statistics on New Enterprises* is restricted to firms with standard ownership types. To ensure valid comparisons, we impose the same sampling conditions on the *General Enterprise Statistics*, *i.e.*, we exclude firms in non-business-related industries and firms with non-standard ownership types.

Third, we use the *Firm Integrated Database (FIDA)*, which identifies all the individuals working in a given firm in the last week of November each year. From this database, we can get information about wages, education, age, and gender of all the workers in a given firm in a given year.

From the FIDA we construct firm-level measures of the average age and wage of the workers, and the gender composition. These variables are based on a worker-level dataset where the information about the firm is linked to each worker. The *FIDA* also allows us to retrieve information on the individuals' educational background from *Statistics Denmark's* education registers. This information is used to characterise the educational content of a job. In the analysis of Section 4, we distinguish between tertiary educations that contain jobs employed by individuals with short further education (13-14 years); medium further education (15-16 years); or long further education (17+ years). This allows us to measure the share of workers who have completed tertiary education.[2]

---

[2] Note that individuals can be associated with more than one firm in a given year as Statistics Denmark records both a primary and (potentially) a secondary job of each individual, where the distinction between the two is based on the wage income generated by the jobs. We discard information about secondary jobs. We deviate from this "one-job-only"-rule in one case: for owners of personally-owned firms with employees. These individuals can have two jobs: As an employer in their own firm and as a wage worker in another firm. However, any given individual can only have one job per firm.

In this analysis, we pay special attention to different kinds of start-ups, that have in common that the founder has been employed in the same (NACE 2-digit) industry prior to starting the company. These companies will be referred to as spinoffs, which is in agreement with the terminology of, e.g., Klepper (2001), Franco and Filson (2006) or Dahl and Reichstein (2007). This definition draws on notions of industry-specific human capital as the prime asset that is transferred to the start-up. It needs to be stressed that there exist a number of different spinoffs definitions in the literature,[3] however, defining spinoffs by founders' industry-experience has the advantage of studies being replicable across different datasets and allows integrating our study into earlier research.

Within the broad spinoff definition being based on industry experience of the founder, we further differentiate between two types of spinoffs: We distinguish spinoffs by whether or not there are more than one individual in the start-up who has been employed in the same firm in t-1.[4] This distinction models the strength of the parent firm – spinoff relationship in terms of worker flows (Eriksson and Kuhn, 2006).[5]

The maximum age of spinoffs in the baseline case is eight years, i.e., spinoffs established in 2002 are eight years of age in 2010. We perform a robustness check where new firms are at most 5 years old. The results are presented in Appendix A.

---

[3] Spinoff definitions differ in the specific kind of assets that are transferred to the spinoff. These assets may by industry-knowledge, as in the present case, business ideas (Bhide, 2000, Fryges et al., 2013) but might also include organizational routines or mutual trust (Helfat and Lieberman, 2002). Also, spinoff definitions based on worker mobility differ in whether they condition on the mobility of the founder(s) alone or groups of individuals (e.g., Eriksson and Kuhn, 2006, Hirakawa et al., 2009, Anderson and Klepper, 2013) moving to the spinoff. The origin of these movers determines whether the spinoff is considered a 'corporate spinoff' (in which case the individuals were in the private sector prior to moving to the spinoff) or an 'academic spinoff' (in which case the individuals were in academic institutions prior to moving to the spinoff). The spinoff definition behind the present study – corporate spinoffs defined by the industry-experience of the founder or the founders – is the most prominent applied in the literature (Garvin, 1983, Arend, 2001, Klepper 2001, 2002, Agarwal et al. 2004, Klepper and Sleeper, 2005, Franco and Filson, 2006, Buenstorf, 2007, Cabral and Wang, 2009).

[4] Specifically, the spin-off definition is based on the founder's industry affiliation in year t-1 being equivalent to the industry of the newly started firm in year t. For a spinoff to be defined as spinoff with more than one person moving from a previous firm to the start-up, more than one of person in the spin-off (possibly but not necessarily including the founder) are required to be registered with the same firm (possibly but not necessarily in the same industry as the spin-off) in t-1. So the spin-off definition is solely based on the founder's industry specific capital, while the definition of 'more than one mover' is solely based on the individuals' previous employer information.

[5] There is a share of start-ups for which Statistic Denmark's algorithm has not succeeded to identify the founder of the firm. These will be integrated in the subsample categorized as 'no spinoff', see Kuhn, Malchow-Møller and Sørensen (2015).

In the analysis, we divide the economy into a number of clusters to try to capture local market conditions. Specifically, we are interested in determining whether a given firm is in a declining or a growing cluster. We measure the local market conditions by the employment growth at the cluster level between 2005 and 2010. The clusters allow comparison of job characteristics not just by whether or not the given job is in a spinoff or not, but also by whether or not the job is in a cluster with growing or declining economic activity in terms of employment.

In the following, we define clusters by the industry and region of the firm. For our baseline cluster definition, we use industries at the 3-digit NACE level, which gives us 233 different industries. Together with five different geographical regions, this results in 1,165 potential clusters.

In the empirical analyses, we use cross sections for 2010 at the firm level, but we use the historical information in the databases to identify the new firms and to construct our industry-region clusters. Before turning to the details of the estimation approach and our empirical findings, we present some descriptive statistics in Tables 2.1 to 2.4 below. In Table 2.1, we present the number of clusters, the number of jobs and the number of firms applied in the analysis, broken down by the employment growth of the clusters. In total, the 1,081 clusters contain approximately 1.56 million jobs and 188,000 firms in 2010.

[Table 2.1 around here]

Table 2.2 splits up the firms on the categories of firms used in this paper: Established firms, non-spinoff entrepreneurial firms, and spinoffs that are further divided into the two spinoff types. Among the 188,000 firms, 80,000 (42 per cent) are identified as new firms, *i.e.*, established after 2001 and hence can be up to eight years old. Approximately 24,000 (13 per cent) are categorised as spinoffs according to our definition, where 11,000 (6 per cent) are categorised as spinoffs with one mover and 13,000 (7 percent) are categorised as spinoffs with more than one mover.

From the lower part of the Table, we can see that while new firms constitute 42 per cent of the firms. They only represent around 16 per cent of the jobs. Most of the jobs (1.31 million) are found in established firms, whereas 170,000 jobs (11 per cent) are found in non-spinoff entrepreneurial firms followed by spinoffs with 82,000 jobs that is further split up into 27,000 jobs in spinoffs with one mover and 55,000 jobs in spinoffs with more than one mover.

[Table 2.2 around here]

Table 2.3 presents the average firm size (as measured by jobs or workers per firm) for the different firm types and by cluster-growth intervals. Established firms have on average 12.1 jobs per firm, whereas the average number of jobs is lower for new firms and in the range between 2.5 and 4.2 jobs per firm.

[Table 2.3 around here]

Table 2.4 summarizes some of the basic characteristics of the workers in the different firm types and by growing and declining clusters, respectively.

[Table 2.4 around here]

3 Estimation Approach

In the analysis, we apply simple linear regression models to compare the productivity levels and characteristics of jobs in spinoffs and other new firms, and to determine how this depends on cluster growth. Specifically, we estimate a number of regressions of the following type:

$$Y = \beta_1 + \beta_2 D^{GC} + \beta_3 D^{SP} + \beta_4 D^{SP} D^{GC} + \gamma X + e$$

where Y is the dependent variable, e.g., the average wage in the firm. X is a vector of control variables, such as age and gender.

We operate with dummy variables for (different types of) new firms and interact them with dummy variables for whether the firm is located in a growing or declining cluster. For ease of exposition, the equation only contains one dummy variable for the firm type, D^{SP}, which equals one for spinoffs and zero for other new firms. Later, D^{SP} is split into two dummy variables for the two spinoff types. Similarly, the dummy variable, D^{GC}, equals 1 for growing clusters and 0 for declining clusters.

In the equation, the parameter β_1 (the constant term) measures the average value of Y in the reference category, which is a non-spinoff entrepreneurial firm in a declining cluster. A non-spinoff entrepreneurial firm in a growing cluster on the other hand is measured by $\beta_1 + \beta_2$, i.e., β_2 measures the difference between a non-spinoff entrepreneurial firm in a growing cluster and a non-spinoff entrepreneurial firm in a declining cluster. The value of a spinoff firm in a declining cluster is given by $\beta_1 + \beta_3$, i.e., β_3 measures the difference between spinoff firms and non-spinoff entrepreneurial firms in a declining cluster. A spinoff firm in a growing cluster is measured by $\beta_1 + \beta_2 + \beta_3 + \beta_4$, i.e., $\beta_3 + \beta_4$ measures the difference between spinoff firms and non-spinoff entrepreneurial firms in a growing cluster, whereas β_4 measures the difference between two differences, namely the difference between spinoffs and non-spinoff entrepreneurial firms in growing clusters and the difference between spinoffs and non-spinoff entrepreneurial firms in declining clusters.

In the following section, we estimate the equation for a number of different dependent variables. In firm-level regressions, we use the average hourly wage, the skill intensity measured as the share of employees with a tertiary education among all employees, and sales per employee. In the latter case, we also control for capital and intermediate inputs to get a measure of firm productivity (TFP).

In each case, we present a number of different regressions. First, we present regressions that only distinguish between types of firms, i.e., we do not take differences between growing and declining clusters into account. This implies that we implicitly impose the restriction $\beta_2 = \beta_4 = 0$ in equation (1). For this regression we compare non-spinoff entrepreneurial firms to spinoffs (but also new firms to old firms). Second, we add the distinction between growing and declining clusters and hence estimate all four parameters (β_1 to β_4). This regression is performed for spinoffs compared to non-spinoff entrepreneurial firms (and for new firms compared to old firms).

Third, we compare non-spinoff entrepreneurial firms to the two types of spinoff firms. The results that we present are for spinoffs with only one person that moves from the origin firm; and spinoffs with more than one person that move from the origin firm to the spinoff. We implicitly impose the restriction $\beta_2 = \beta_4 = 0$ in equation (1) and we also add the distinction between growing and declining clusters and hence estimate all four parameters (β_1 to β_4).

Fourth, we include controls for the age, gender and education level of the worker(s) – except in the case where the dependent variable is the education level of the workers. In neither of the regressions discussed so far do we include additional control variables. By including this information, we take worker heterogeneity into account when comparing job characteristics of different firms. If this is an important aspect, the estimated firm-type dummies are expected to be of less importance after controlling for these worker characteristics. We also include industry and region dummies thereby taking (potentially unobserved) differences across industries and regions into account. If, e.g., certain industries or regions tend to have high employment growth, the dummy variable for growing clusters will become less important as part of the variation will now be picked up by the industry and region dummies.

Fifth, we take this one step further and include cluster dummies, implying that we control for observed and unobserved differences at the cluster level. This regression thereby yields within-cluster differences between spinoff and non-spinoff entrepreneurial firms. As a consequence, β_2 cannot be estimated in this regression. If the differences in job characteristics types of new firms on different (unobserved) cluster characteristics, the estimated difference between types of new firms will become smaller in this case.

4 Results

In this section, we focus on the characteristics of the jobs within different types of firms; established, new firms, and spinoffs. Our main focus is on the comparison between spinoff firms and non-spinoff firms, i.e., we investigate whether the job characteristics of spinoffs are different from those in non-spinoff entrepreneurial firms.

As our first measure of job quality, we use the wage rate. In Table 4.1, we therefore present the results of estimating (1) using the log of the average hourly wage as the dependent variable. As some firms do not have employees, and since wage information is not reliable for all firms with employees, the sample is reduced to around 95,000 observations (firms) in this case (out of a total of 188,000 firms); the number of new firms is around 30,000 observations (out of around 80,000 new firms).[6]

[Table 4.1 around here]

In column 1, all firms – old and new – are included in the regression with a dummy for new firm included. In this case, we find that new firms pay slightly higher average wages (around 2 per cent) than old firms. In column 2, we condition on the cluster growth by including the dummy for positive employment growth in the cluster, D^{GC}, and its interaction with the new-firm dummy. In this case, we can estimate all the four beta coefficients from equation (1). We find that average wages of old firms is lower in declining clusters than in growing clusters, as β_2 is significantly positive. New firms,

---

[6] Statistics Denmark's hourly wage variable is based on the available information from the wage income registers and different sources of information to determine working hours. The measurement of the latter can easily become highly uncertain, for which reason Statistics Denmark attaches a quality estimate to its hourly wage variable. If this estimate makes the wage information of a given individual too doubtful, the given individual's wage record is not considered for the analysis.

on the other hand, now exhibit wages slightly lower than established firms in declining clusters (β_3 is negative) and higher than established firms (around 7%) in growing clusters ($\beta_3 + \beta_4$ is positive). In other words, the local business environment does seem to make a difference for the relative performance of new vs. old firms.

In the following columns, we compare spinoffs to non-spinoff entrepreneurial firms and exclude established firms from the regressions. In columns 3 and 4 it is seen that there is no significant differences between spinoffs and non-spinoff entrepreneurial firms, except for spinoffs having higher wages of a magnitude of 3 percent in growing clusters. In column 5, it is seen that it makes a difference to distinguish spinoffs in the number of persons moving from the origin firm to the spinoff. For spinoffs where more than one person move from the origin firm to the spinoff the average wage rate is lower than in non-spinoff entrepreneurial firms, whereas the wage rate is higher in spinoffs where only one person moves. This result is qualified in column 6 where we condition on cluster growth by including the dummy for positive employment growth in the cluster, D^{GC}, and its interaction with spinoff dummies. In this case, it is seen that the wage differences are mainly present in growing clusters, whereas there are almost no wage differences in declining clusters.

We check for the robustness of column 6 by including additional controls. In column 7, we control for the share of women among the workers, the share of workers with a tertiary education degree, and the average age among workers. In addition, we include industry and region dummies. The inclusion of these variables results in different results. Now, both spinoff types have higher wages than non-spinoff entrepreneurial firms. Spinoffs with more than one person moving from the origin firm actually pay higher wages in both growing and declining clusters, and the wage difference is around 4 per cent (β_{32}), whereas the difference is around 2 per cent (β_{31}) in declining clusters and around 6 per cent ($\beta_{31} + \beta_{41}$) in growing clusters for spinoffs with one person moving from the origin firm.

Finally, columns 8 include industry x region dummies that corresponds to fixed effects at the cluster level. In this case the results from column 7 carry through. That is, we still observe higher average wages in both types of spinoffs when we control for (possibly unobserved) industry- and region-specific characteristics. In other words, within a cluster, we still observe higher average wages in spinoffs compared to non-spinoff entrepreneurial firms.

In Table 4.2, we consider the skill intensity, where we use the share of employees in the firm with a tertiary education degree as the dependent variable. For this Table all firms enter the regressions; the sample size almost doubles for all firms in columns 1-2 and more than doubles for new firms in columns 3-8 compared to Table 4.1.

[Table 4.2 around here]

According to the first column of Table 4.2, the unconditional skill-intensity is 2 percentage points higher in new firms than in old firms (the estimate of β_3 is both positive and significantly different from zero). When distinguishing between growing and declining clusters, it is found that the education-intensity is around 10 percentage points higher in old firms in growing clusters compared to old firms in declining clusters, as the estimate of β_2 equals 0.098. Moreover, new firms are found to be more education-intensive than old firms – both in declining clusters (0.4 percentage points) and especially in growing clusters (0.4 + 2.4 = 2.8 percentage points).

Turning to the comparison between spinoffs and non-spinoff entrepreneurial firms in columns 3 and 4, it is seen that spinoffs are less skills intensive when cluster growth is not taken into account. However, there is a positive difference between spinoffs and non-spinoff entrepreneurial firms in growing clusters and a negative difference in declining clusters, which is seen in column 4.

When distinguishing between spinoff types in columns 5 and 6, it is found that spinoffs where more than one person moves to the spinoff from the origin firm are less skill intensive than other new firms. Moreover, it is found that spinoffs where one person only moves are more skill intensive but only in growing clusters.

Controlling for worker heterogeneity and including industry and region dummies in column 7, change this picture since now spinoffs independent of type become more skill intensive than non-spinoff entrepreneurial firms in growing clusters. When looking at within cluster differences in column 8, we still find that spinoffs have higher skill intensity – around 2-2.5 percentage points – compared to non-spinoff entrepreneurial firms in growing clusters.

In Table 4.3, we present the results for the case where the dependent variable is the (log of) sales (or revenue) per worker. From column 1, we can see that sales per worker are, in general, lower in new firms (16 per cent) when compared to established firms. When we distinguish between growing and declining clusters (column 2), we still find that new firms have lower sales per worker – and there is no difference between declining and growing clusters (the estimate of β_4 is insignificant).

[Table 4.3 around here]

Turning to the comparison between spinoffs and non-spinoff entrepreneurial firms, we find that sales per worker are much larger in spinoffs compared to non-spinoff entrepreneurial firms. In column 3, it is found that spinoffs have 25 percent higher than other new firms ($\exp(\beta_3) - 1 = \exp(0.225) - 1 = 0.25$). When distinguishing cluster growth, we find that labour productivity is 16 percent higher in declining clusters and 34 percent higher in growing clusters ($\exp(\beta_3 + \beta_4) - 1 = \exp(0.150 + 0.142) - 1 = 0.34$).

When distinguishing between spinoff type in columns 5 and 6, we find that spinoffs with more than one person moving from the origin firm are 28 percent more productive than non-spinoff entrepreneurial firms ($\exp(\beta_3) - 1 = \exp(0.247) - 1 = 0.28$). The picture of spinoffs being more productive compared to other new firms is rediscovered in column 6 with the modification that firms located in growing clusters are more productive. Controlling for worker heterogeneity and fixed effects (columns 7-8) modifies this conclusion since the higher sales per worker in spinoffs with more than one mover is independent across growing and declining clusters.

Table 4.4 also has (the log of) sales per worker as the dependent variable, but includes (the log of) capital per worker, intermediate inputs per worker and number of workers as additional controls. In this case, the estimates of β_1 to β_4 can be interpreted as (differences in) total factor productivity. In column 1, we can see that this results in new firms having slightly higher TFP (1.5 percent) than old firms on average. When distinguishing between growing and declining clusters (column 2), it turns out that the "advantage" of new firms is larger within growing clusters as the estimated sum of β_3 and β_4 amounts to 5 per cent), whereas the estimate of β_3 is small, positive and only significant at the 10 percent significance level, implying that new firms in declining clusters have slightly higher TFP (1 per cent) than old firms.

When we turn to the comparison between spinoffs and spin-off new firms in columns 3 and 4, it is found that spinoffs are more productive. The difference is around 10 percent; and higher in growing than in declining clusters. The productivity advantage holds even when controlling for worker heterogeneity and cluster fixed effects (column 8). It should be observed that there are no large differences between the two spinoff types.[7]

[Table 4.4 around here]

In sum, we find that spinoffs on average have higher wages, are more skill intensive, have higher sales per worker and are more productive than non-spinoff entrepreneurial firms. This is case even when we control worker heterogeneity and industry and region clusters characteristics. Furthermore, we find that the results carry through for both types of spinoffs without much variation.

As a robustness check of our results, we have re-estimated the tables of Section 4, where we define new firms as those established after 2005, instead of all firms established after 2001. The results are presented in Appendix A. This reduces the number of new firms in the analysis from around 80,000 to 60,000 of which around 20,000 are new spinoffs. Using this definition of new firms, we find very similar results to those of Section 4. We have also experimented with investigating the characteristics of jobs in spinoffs in manufacturing and service firms. We do not present the results here. However, only very few spinoff firms around 3,200 firms exist in manufacturing. The overall impression from this analysis is that spinoffs in manufacturing are relatively similar to non-spinoff entrepreneurial firms in manufacturing.

5 Conclusion

This paper investigates whether the quality of jobs in spinoff entrepreneurs are higher than for other entrepreneurs. The purpose of the analysis is to investigate whether corporate spinoffs are important drivers of industry dynamics. Identifying characteristics of successful start-ups is an important task in the understanding of the characterization of spinoffs.

Spinoffs, defined in different ways, have in numerous studies been shown to be successful in terms of survival (e.g., Phillips 2002, Agarwal et al. 2004, Dahl and Reichstein 2007), profitability (Dahl and Sorenson, 2014), or innovation (Agarwal et al., 2004). We contribute to the literature by investigating the quality of jobs in spinoffs as measured by average wages in firms, skill intensities, sales by worker and productivity. Moreover, we contribute to the literature by using organic new

---

[7] Note that throughout Table 4.4, the coefficients of capital per worker and input per worker are as expected, whereas the coefficient of (the log of) the number of workers is found to be significantly positive, which indicates increasing returns to scale.

firms as unit of measurement for entrepreneurship. This is different from standard measures of entrepreneurs that are measured by firm or establishment age.

Firms are spinoffs if the founder of a new firm has been employed in the same industry prior to starting the company. This definition draws on notions of industry-specific human capital as the prime asset that is transferred to the start-up. However, it needs to be stressed that there exist a number of different spinoffs definitions in the literature.

The analyses are based on Danish worker-firm register data for the time period 2001-2010, which cover almost the entire private sector of the Danish economy. Several results are established in the paper. First, we find that around one third of new firms are spinoff. Second, we find that spinoffs on average have higher wages, are more skill intensive, have higher sales per worker and are more productive than non-spinoff entrepreneurial firms. This is case even when we control worker heterogeneity and industry and region clusters characteristics.

Kuhn, Malchow-Møller and Sørensen (2015) find that new firms have similar average wages, similar skill intensity and are more productive compared to old firms. Combined with the findings of the present analysis this implies that spinoff entrepreneurs create jobs of higher quality compared to old jobs. In this sense, spinoff entrepreneurs are important for industry dynamics.

The broader perspective of the results presented in this paper is that jobs in organic spinoffs are high quality jobs in the sense that they pay higher wages, have higher skill content, and – in particular – are more productive; both measured by labour productivity and TFP. These results indicate that spinoffs do play an important role as an engine for growth and prosperity.

References

Agarwal, R., R. Echambadi, A. M. Franco and M. B. Sarkar (2004), Knowledge transfer through inheritance: spinout generation, development and survival, Academy of Management Journal, 47(4), 501–522.

Anderson, M. and S. Klepper (2013), "Characteristics and performance of new firms and spinoffs in Sweden", *Industrial and Corporate Change*, 22 (1), 245-280

Arend, R. (2001), "When Firms originate from within", *Small Business Economics*, 16, 205-222

Buenstorf, G. (2007), "Evolution on the Shoulders of Giants: Entrepreneurship and Firm Survival in the German Laser Industry", *Review of Industrial Organization*, 30, 179-202

Cabral, L., and Z. Wang (2009), "Spinoffs: Theory and Evidence from the Early U.S. Automobile Industry," Working Paper RWP 08-15 (revised version July 2009), The Federal Reserve Bank of Kansas City, Kansas City, MO.

Callan, B. (2001), "Generating spinoffs: evidence from across the OECD", In OECD, STI review N026: Special Issue on Fostering High-tech Spinoffs: A Public Strategy for Innovation. OECD, Paris.

Cooper, A.C. (1985), "The role of incubator organizations in the founding of growth-oriented firms", *Journal of Business Venturing*, 1, 75–86.

Dahl, M. S., and T. Reichstein (2007), "Are You Experienced? Prior Experience and the Survival of New Organizations", *Industry and Innovation*, 14 (5), 497-511.

Dahl, M.S. and O. Sorenson (2014), "The who, why, and how of spinoffs", *Industrial and Corporate Change*, 23(3), 661-688.

Eriksson, T. and J. Kuhn (2006), "Firm spinoffs in Denmark 1981-2000 - patterns of entry and exit", *International Journal of Industrial Organization*, 24(5), 1021-1040

Franco, A. M., and D. Filson (2006), "Spinouts: Knowledge Diffusion through Employee Mobility", *The Rand Journal of Economics*, 37 (4), 841-860

Fryges, H., B. Müller, M. Niefert (2014), "Job machine, think tank, or both: what makes corporate spinoffs different?", *Small Business Economics*, 43 (2), 369-391

Garvin, D. A. (1983), "Spinoffs and the New Firm Formation Process", *California Management Review*, 25 (2), 3-20

Helfat, C. E., and M. B. Lieberman (2002), "The Birth of Capabilities: Market Entry and the Importance of Pre-History", *Industrial and Corporate Change*, 11 (4), 725-760

Hirakawa O. T., M.-A. Muendler, J. Rauch (2009), "Employee spinoffs and other entrants: stylized facts from Brazil", NBER Working Paper # 15638.

Klepper, S. (2001), "Employee Start-ups in High-Tech Industries", *Industrial and Corporate Change*, 10 (3), 639-674.

Kuhn, J.M., N. Malchow-Møller, A. Sørensen (2015), "New Firms vs. Old Firms: Who Create the Better Jobs?", mimeo Copenhagen Business School

Phillips, D. J. (2002), "A Genealogical Approach to Organizational Life Chances: The Parent-Progeny Transfer among Silicon Valley Law Firms, 1946-1996", *Administrative Science Quarterly*, 47, 474-506.

Roberts, P. W., S. Klepper, S. Hayward (2011), "Founder backgrounds and the evolution of firm size", *Industrial and Corporate Change*, 20(6), 1515-1538.

Van Praag, C.M., and P.H. Versloot (2007), "What is the value of entrepreneurship? A review of recent research", *Small Business Economics*, 29 (4), 351-382

TABLE 2.1.: Number of clusters and jobs. By cluster growth

Cluster growth	Number of clusters		Number of jobs		Number of firms	
	#	%	#	%	#	%
-0.50-	124	11.47	38,334	2.46	4,314	2.29
-0.50;-0.25	202	18.69	222,933	14.29	19,820	10.54
-0.25;-0.1	190	17.58	366,298	23.47	47,918	25.48
-0.1-0.1	253	23.40	634,579	40.67	76,068	40.45
0.1-0.25	85	7.86	121,984	7.82	19,838	10.55
0.25-0.5	65	6.01	113,097	7.25	14,610	7.77
0.5+ New	162	14.99	63,227	4.05	5,476	2.91
Totals	1,081	100.00	1,560,452	100.00	188,044	100.00

TABLE 2.2: Number of firm types and jobs. By cluster growth and firm types

Number of firms

Cluster growth	Established firms #	Established firms %	Non-spinoff new firms #	Non-spinoff new firms %	Spinoffs #	Spinoffs %	Spinoffs, one mover #	Spinoffs, one mover %	Spinoffs, more than one mover #	Spinoffs, more than one mover %
-0.50-	2,439	2.3	1,439	2.6	436	1.8	192	1.8	244	1.9
-0.50;-0.25	11,925	11.0	5,558	10.0	2,337	9.7	1,040	9.5	1,297	9.9
-0.25;-0.1	28,360	26.2	11,486	20.6	8,072	33.6	3,546	32.5	4,526	34.5
-0.1-0.1	44,954	41.5	22,230	39.9	8,884	37.0	3,929	36.0	4,955	37.8
0.1-0.25	10,997	10.2	6,674	12.0	2,167	9.0	1,062	9.7	1,105	8.4
0.25-0.5	7,092	6.5	5,765	10.4	1,753	7.3	927	8.5	826	6.3
0.5+	2,565	2.4	2,543	4.6	368	1.5	213	2.0	155	1.2
Totals	108,332	100.0	55,695	100.0	24,017	100.0	10,909	100.0	13,108	100.0

Number of jobs

Cluster growth	Established firms #	Established firms %	Non-spinoff new firms #	Non-spinoff new firms %	Spinoffs #	Spinoffs %	Spinoffs, one mover #	Spinoffs, one mover %	Spinoffs, more than one mover #	Spinoffs, more than one mover %
-0.50-	31,250	2.4	5,042	3.0	2,042	2.5	582	2.1	1,460	2.7
-0.50;-0.25	195,994	15.0	18,926	11.2	8,013	9.8	2,461	9.1	5,552	10.1
-0.25;-0.1	308,057	23.5	33,283	19.7	24,958	30.4	7,669	28.2	17,289	31.4
-0.1-0.1	535,104	40.9	66,153	39.1	33,322	40.6	10,604	39.1	22,718	41.3
0.1-0.25	94,782	7.2	19,698	11.6	7,504	9.1	3,068	11.3	4,436	8.1
0.25-0.5	92,587	7.1	15,268	9.0	5,242	6.4	2,265	8.3	2,977	5.4
0.5+	51,228	3.9	10,914	6.4	1,085	1.3	498	1.8	587	1.1
Totals	1,309,002	100.0	169,284	100.0	82,166	100.0	27,147	100.0	55,019	100.0

TABLE 2.3: Average number of jobs per firm. By cluster growth after firm types

Cluster growth	Jobs per firm				
	Established firms #	Non-spinoff new firm #	Spinoffs #	Spinoffs, one mover #	Spinoffs, more than one mover #
-0.50-	12.8	3.5	4.7	3.0	6.0
-0.50;-0.25	16.4	3.4	3.4	2.4	4.3
-0.25;-0.1	10.9	2.9	3.1	2.2	3.8
-0.1-0.1	11.9	3.0	3.8	2.7	4.6
0.1-0.25	8.6	3.0	3.5	2.9	4.0
0.25-0.5	13.1	2.6	3.0	2.4	3.6
0.5+	20.0	4.3	2.9	2.3	3.8
Totals	12.1	3.0	3.4	2.5	4.2

Table 2.4: Average individual characteristics. By firm type and cluster growth

Cluster growth	Firm type	Number of workers	Number of firms	Mean age	Share of females	Share of highly educated	Mean hourly wage (DKK)
Negative	Established firms	810,103	71,316	41	0.32	0.04	211.69
Negative	Other new firms	95,116	30,989	38	0.31	0.04	191.20
Negative	Spin-offs	55,271	16,272	36	0.30	0.02	170.57
Negative	Spin-offs, type 1	16,981	7,064	37	0.28	0.03	171.65
Negative	Spin-offs, type 2	38,290	9,208	36	0.30	0.02	170.16
Positive	Established firms	498,899	37,016	38	0.42	0.11	224.28
Positive	Other new firms	74,168	24,706	37	0.39	0.12	203.62
Positive	Spin-offs	26,895	7,745	36	0.39	0.11	193.38
Positive	Spin-offs, type 1	10,166	3,845	37	0.37	0.13	207.99
Positive	Spin-offs, type 2	16,729	3,900	35	0.40	0.11	185.39

TABLE 4.1: Average Wages in New and Old Firms, Firm Level, 2010

	(1)	(2)	(3)	(4)	(5)	(6)	(7)	(8)
Constant (β_1)	5.106***	5.102***	5.092***	5.059***	5.092***	5.059***	4.753***	4.803***
	(0.002)	(0.002)	(0.004)	(0.005)	(0.004)	(0.005)	(0.102)	(0.024)
Positive cluster growth (β_2)		0.016***		0.086***		0.086***	-0.023**	
		(0.005)		(0.009)		(0.009)	(0.010)	
Firm types:								
New firm (β_3)	0.022***	-0.008**						
	(0.003)	(0.004)						
Spinoff (β_3)			0.008	0.003				
			(0.006)	(0.007)				
Spinoff type 1 (β_{31})					0.057***	0.017*	0.019**	0.019**
					(0.008)	(0.009)	(0.009)	(0.009)
Spinoff type 2 (β_{32})					-0.022***	-0.005	0.044***	0.042***
					(0.007)	(0.007)	(0.007)	(0.008)
Firm type x Positive cluster growth:								
Positive cluster growth x New firm (β_4)		0.081***						
		(0.008)						
Positive cluster growth x Spinoff (β_4)				0.033**				
				(0.014)				
Positive cluster growth x Spinoff type 1 (β_4)						0.118***	0.044***	0.039**
						(0.018)	(0.016)	(0.015)
Positive cluster growth x Spinoff type 2 (β_4)						-0.034**	-0.004	-0.005
						(0.016)	(0.014)	(0.018)
Controls for gender, age and education	no	no	no	no	no	no	yes	yes
Industry and Region fixed effects	no	no	no	no	no	no	yes	no
Industry x Region (= cluster) fixed effects	no	no	no	no	no	no	no	yes
Observations	95,228	95,228	29,445	29,445	29,445	29,445	29,445	29,445
R-squared	0.000	0.004	0.000	0.009	0.002	0.013	0.280	0.043

Notes: The dependent variable is the log of the average hourly wage in the firm. The sample is reduced to around 95,000 firms/30,000 new firms and the number of clusters to 1054, because some firms do not have employees and because reliable wage information cannot be obtained for all firms with employees. See text for more details. Robust standard errors in parentheses. The R-squared in column 5 is computed on the de-meaned data. *** p<0.01, ** p<0.05, * p<0.1.

TABLE 4.2: Skill-Intensity in New and Old Firms, Firm Level, 2010

	(1)	(2)	(3)	(4)	(5)	(6)	(7)	(8)
Constant (β_1)	0.071***	0.037***	0.093***	0.042***	0.093***	0.042***	-0.059***	0.032**
	(0.001)	(0.001)	(0.001)	(0.001)	(0.001)	(0.001)	(0.009)	(0.016)
Positive cluster growth (β_2)		0.098***		0.114***		0.114***	0.015***	
		(0.002)		(0.003)		(0.003)	(0.003)	
Firm types:								
New firm (β_3)	0.020***	0.004***						
	(0.001)	(0.001)						
Spinoff (β_3)			-0.016***	-0.014***				
			(0.002)	(0.002)				
Spinoff type 1 (β_{31})					0.001	-0.007***	0.004*	0.004
					(0.003)	(0.002)	(0.002)	(0.003)
Spinoff type 2 (β_{32})					-0.030***	-0.020***	-0.001	-0.003
					(0.002)	(0.002)	(0.002)	(0.002)
Firm type x Positive cluster growth:								
Positive cluster growth x New firm (β_4)		0.024***						
		(0.003)						
Positive cluster growth x Spinoff (β_4)				0.040***				
				(0.005)				
Positive cluster growth x Spinoff type 1 (β_4)						0.055***	0.027***	0.023**
						(0.007)	(0.006)	(0.010)
Positive cluster growth x Spinoff type 2 (β_4)						0.024***	0.019***	0.021**
						(0.006)	(0.005)	(0.011)
Controls for gender, age and education	no	no	no	no	no	no	yes	yes
Industry and Region fixed effects	no	no	no	no	no	no	yes	no
Industry x Region (= cluster) fixed effects	no	no	no	no	no	no	no	yes
Observations	188,044	188,044	70,654	70,654	70,654	70,654	70,421	70,421
R-squared	0.002	0.049	0.001	0.055	0.002	0.056	0.225	0.004

Notes: The dependent variable is the the share of employees with a tertiary education degree in the firm. The number of clusters is 1081, since some clusteres do not contain any observations in 2010. See text for more details. Robust standard errors in parentheses. The R-squared in column 5 is computed on the de-meaned data. *** p<0.01, ** p<0.05, * p<0.1.

TABLE 4.3: Sales per Worker in New and Old Firms, Firm Level, 2010

	(1)	(2)	(3)	(4)	(5)	(6)	(7)	(8)
Constant (β_1)	13.404***	13.469***	13.112***	13.214***	13.112***	13.214***	13.812***	13.041***
	(0.003)	(0.003)	(0.004)	(0.005)	(0.004)	(0.005)	(0.135)	(0.022)
Positive cluster growth (β_2)		-0.193***		-0.227***		-0.227***	-0.032***	
		(0.006)		(0.008)		(0.008)	(0.010)	
Firm types:								
New firm (β_3)	-0.158***	-0.143***						
	(0.004)	(0.005)						
Spinoff (β_3)			0.225***	0.150***				
			(0.007)	(0.008)				
Spinoff type 1 (β_{31})					0.199***	0.125***	0.136***	0.131***
					(0.009)	(0.011)	(0.010)	(0.015)
Spinoff type 2 (β_{32})					0.247***	0.169***	0.151***	0.142***
					(0.008)	(0.010)	(0.009)	(0.012)
Firm type x Positive cluster growth:								
Positive cluster growth x New firm (β_4)		-0.004						
		(0.009)						
Positive cluster growth x Spinoff (β_4)				0.142***				
				(0.014)				
Positive cluster growth x Spinoff type 1 (β_4)						0.147***	0.064***	0.069***
						(0.019)	(0.016)	(0.025)
Positive cluster growth x Spinoff type 2 (β_4)						0.143***	0.016	0.027
						(0.018)	(0.016)	(0.026)
Controls for gender, age and education	no	no	no	no	no	no	yes	yes
Industry and Region fixed effects	no	no	no	no	no	no	yes	no
Industry x Region (= cluster) fixed effects	no	no	no	no	no	no	no	yes
Observations	178,152	178,152	67,431	67,431	67,431	67,431	67,228	67,228
R-squared	0.008	0.020	0.016	0.028	0.016	0.029	0.267	0.014

Notes: The dependent variable is the log of sales (revenue) per worker. The number of clusters is 1021, since some clusters do not contain any observations in 2010. See text for more details. Robust standard errors in parentheses. The R-squared in column 5 is computed on the de-meaned data.
*** $p<0.01$, ** $p<0.05$, * $p<0.1$.

TABLE 4.4: Productivity in New and Old Firms, 2010

	(1)	(2)	(3)	(4)	(5)	(6)	(7)	(8)
Constant (β_1)	7.051***	6.977***	7.059***	6.957***	7.057***	6.956***	6.582***	6.735***
	(0.022)	(0.022)	(0.034)	(0.034)	(0.034)	(0.034)	(0.108)	(0.101)
Positive cluster growth (β_2)		0.052***		0.079***		0.080***	-0.022**	
		(0.005)		(0.007)		(0.007)	(0.009)	
Firm types:								
New firm (β_3)	0.015***	-0.010**						
	(0.003)	(0.004)						
Spinoff (β_3)			0.109***	0.092***				
			(0.006)	(0.006)				
Spinoff type 1 (β_{31})					0.121***	0.093***	0.085***	0.081***
					(0.008)	(0.009)	(0.008)	(0.009)
Spinoff type 2 (β_{32})					0.098***	0.091***	0.081***	0.074***
					(0.007)	(0.008)	(0.007)	(0.007)
Firm type x Positive cluster growth:								
Positive cluster growth x New firm (β_4)		0.065***						
		(0.007)						
Positive cluster growth x Spinoff (β_4)				0.076***				
				(0.013)				
Positive cluster growth x Spinoff type 1 (β_4)						0.103***	0.039**	0.045**
						(0.017)	(0.016)	(0.020)
Positive cluster growth x Spinoff type 2 (β_4)						0.051***	0.033**	0.046**
						(0.016)	(0.014)	(0.023)
log_kob_emp	0.397***	0.402***	0.354***	0.361***	0.354***	0.361***	0.356***	0.355***
	(0.002)	(0.002)	(0.003)	(0.003)	(0.003)	(0.003)	(0.003)	(0.015)
log_kap_emp	0.117***	0.116***	0.160***	0.158***	0.160***	0.158***	0.171***	0.172***
	(0.001)	(0.001)	(0.002)	(0.002)	(0.002)	(0.002)	(0.003)	(0.009)
log_emp	0.059***	0.058***	0.036***	0.036***	0.038***	0.037***	0.074***	0.074***
	(0.001)	(0.001)	(0.003)	(0.003)	(0.003)	(0.003)	(0.003)	(0.008)
Controls for gender, age and education	no	no	no	no	no	no	yes	yes
Industry and Region fixed effects	no	no	no	no	no	no	yes	no
Industry x Region (= cluster) fixed effects	no	no	no	no	no	no	no	yes
Observations	133,087	133,087	48,827	48,827	48,827	48,827	48,688	48,688
R-squared	0.527	0.530	0.488	0.492	0.488	0.492	0.583	0.467

Notes: The dependent variable is the log of sales (revenue) per worker in the firm. See text for more details. Robust standard errors in parentheses. The R-squared in column 5 is computed on the de-meaned data. The number of clusters is 975. *** p<0.01, ** p<0.05, * p<0.1.

Appendix A. Estimation Results for Alternative Definition of Entrepreneurs (Max age of 5 years).

Include Tables A2.1-A4.4

TABLE A2.1.: Number of clusters and jobs. By cluster growth

Cluster growth	Number of clusters		Number of jobs		Number of firms	
	#	%	#	%	#	%
-0.50-	124	11.47	38,334	2.46	4,314	2.29
-0.50;-0.25	202	18.69	222,933	14.29	19,820	10.54
-0.25;-0.1	190	17.58	366,298	23.47	47,918	25.48
-0.1-0.1	253	23.40	634,579	40.67	76,068	40.45
0.1-0.25	85	7.86	121,984	7.82	19,838	10.55
0.25-0.5	65	6.01	113,097	7.25	14,610	7.77
0.5+	162		63,227		5,476	2.91
New						
Totals	1,081	85.01	1,560,452	95.95	188,044	100.00

TABLE A2.2: Number of firm types and jobs. By cluster growth and firm types

Number of firms

Cluster growth	Established firms		Other New firms		Spinoffs		Spinoffs, one		Spinoffs, two	
	#	%	#	%	#	%	#	%	#	%
-0.50-	2,952	2.3	1,072	2.6	290	1.7	118	1.7	172	1.7
-0.50:-0.25	14,271	11.0	3,970	9.7	1,579	9.3	627	9.1	952	9.4
-0.25:-0.1	33,790	26.0	8,370	20.4	5,758	33.8	2,202	32.0	3,556	35.0
-0.1-0.1	53,597	41.2	16,241	39.7	6,230	36.6	2,433	35.4	3,797	37.4
0.1-0.25	13,489	10.4	4,810	11.7	1,539	9.0	675	9.8	864	8.5
0.25-0.5	8,866	6.8	4,412	10.8	1,332	7.8	647	9.4	685	6.7
0.5+	3,091	2.4	2,071	5.1	314	1.8	178	2.6	136	1.3
Totals	130,056	100.0	40,946	100.0	17,042	100.0	6,880	100.0	10,162	100.0

Number of jobs

Cluster growth	Established firms		Other New firms		Spinoffs		Spinoffs, one		Spinoffs, two	
	#	%	#	%	#	%	#	%	#	%
-0.50-	33,989	2.4	3,421	3.4	924	1.9	236	1.7	688	2.0
-0.50:-0.25	208,303	14.8	10,296	10.2	4,334	9.0	1,345	9.7	2,989	8.7
-0.25:-0.1	331,488	23.5	20,032	19.8	14,778	30.7	4,026	28.9	10,752	31.5
-0.1-0.1	573,275	40.6	41,197	40.8	20,107	41.8	5,546	39.9	14,561	42.6
0.1-0.25	107,297	7.6	10,774	10.7	3,913	8.1	1,272	9.1	2,641	7.7
0.25-0.5	101,021	7.2	8,849	8.8	3,227	6.7	1,159	8.3	2,068	6.1
0.5+	56,022	4.0	6,413	6.4	792	1.6	328	2.4	464	1.4
Totals	1,411,395	100.0	100,982	100.0	48,075	100.0	13,912	100.0	34,163	100.0

TABLE A2.3: Average number of jobs per firm. By cluster growth after firm types

Cluster growth	Jobs per firm			Spinoffs, type 1	Spinoffs, type 2
	Established firms #	Other New firms #	Spin-offs #	#	#
-0.50-	11.5	3.2	3.2	2.0	4.0
-0.50;-0.25	14.6	2.6	2.7	2.1	3.1
-0.25;-0.1	9.8	2.4	2.6	1.8	3.0
-0.1-0.1	10.7	2.5	3.2	2.3	3.8
0.1-0.25	8.0	2.2	2.5	1.9	3.1
0.25-0.5	11.4	2.0	2.4	1.8	3.0
0.5+	18.1	3.1	2.5	1.8	3.4
Totals	10.9	2.5	2.8	2.0	3.4

Table A2.4: Average individual characteristics. By firm type and cluster growth

Cluster growth	Firm type	Number of workers	Number of firms	Mean age	Share of females	Share of highly educated	Mean hourly wage (DKK)
Negative	Established firms	870,999	84,661	40.48	0.32	0.04	210.39
Negative	Other new firms	57,269	22,529	37.18	0.31	0.04	185.18
Negative	Spin-offs	32,222	11,387	35.34	0.29	0.02	164.63
Negative	Spin-offs, type 1	8,767	4,320	35.61	0.26	0.03	167.74
Negative	Spin-offs, type 2	23,455	7,067	35.24	0.31	0.02	163.66
Positive	Established firms	540,396	45,395	38.06	0.41	0.11	223.36
Positive	Other new firms	43,713	18,417	37.09	0.39	0.12	195.72
Positive	Spin-offs	15,853	5,655	35.74	0.39	0.12	180.50
Positive	Spin-offs, type 1	5,145	2,560	37.15	0.37	0.15	202.31
Positive	Spin-offs, type 2	10,708	3,095	35.04	0.40	0.11	171.16

TABLE A4.1: Average Wages in New and Old Firms, Firm Level, 2010

	(1)	(2)	(3)	(4)	(5)	(6)	(7)	(8)
Constant (β_1)	5.112***	5.103***	5.084***	5.049***	5.084***	5.049***	4.793***	4.764***
	(0.002)	(0.002)	(0.005)	(0.006)	(0.005)	(0.006)	(0.057)	(0.025)
Positive cluster growth (β_2)		0.030***		0.092***		0.092***	-0.014	
		(0.004)		(0.011)		(0.011)	(0.013)	
Firm types:								
New firm (β_3)	0.009**	-0.019***						
	(0.004)	(0.004)						
Spinoff (β_3)			0.010	0.005				
			(0.008)	(0.008)				
Spinoff type 1 (β_{31})					0.081***	0.034***	0.032***	0.030***
					(0.011)	(0.012)	(0.011)	(0.011)
Spinoff type 2 (β_{32})					-0.027***	-0.008	0.044***	0.041***
					(0.008)	(0.009)	(0.008)	(0.009)
Firm type x Positive cluster growth:								
Positive cluster growth x New firm (β_4)		0.071***						
		(0.009)						
Positive cluster growth x Spinoff (β_4)				0.031*				
				(0.017)				
Positive cluster growth x Spinoff type 1 (β_4)						0.131***	0.034*	0.032
						(0.023)	(0.020)	(0.020)
Positive cluster growth x Spinoff type 2 (β_4)						-0.038*	-0.014	-0.012
						(0.020)	(0.017)	(0.020)
Controls for gender, age and education	no	no	no	no	no	no	yes	yes
Industry and Region fixed effects	no	no	no	no	no	no	yes	no
Industry x Region (= cluster) fixed effects	no	no	no	no	no	no	no	yes
Observations	95,228	95,228	19,741	19,741	19,741	19,741	19,741	19,741
R-squared	0.000	0.003	0.000	0.009	0.004	0.015	0.282	0.047

Notes: The dependent variable is the log of the average hourly wage in the firm. The sample is reduced to around 95,000 firms/30,000 new firms and the number of clusters to 1054, because some firms do not have employees and because reliable wage information cannot be obtained for all firms with employees. See text for more details. Robust standard errors in parentheses. The R-squared in column 5 is computed on the de-meaned data. *** p<0.01, ** p<0.05, * p<0.1.

TABLE A4.2: Skill-Intensity in New and Old Firms, Firm Level, 2010

	(1)	(2)	(3)	(4)	(5)	(6)	(7)	(8)
Constant (β_1)	0.073***	0.038***	0.096***	0.044***	0.096***	0.044***	-0.068***	0.035**
	(0.001)	(0.001)	(0.002)	(0.001)	(0.002)	(0.001)	(0.009)	(0.016)
Positive cluster growth (β_2)		0.101***		0.115***		0.115***	0.016***	
		(0.002)		(0.003)		(0.003)	(0.004)	
Firm types:								
New firm (β_3)	0.020***	0.003***						
	(0.001)	(0.001)						
Spinoff (β_3)			-0.015***	-0.016***				
			(0.002)	(0.002)				
Spinoff type 1 (β_{31})					0.007*	-0.007**	0.006**	0.006
					(0.004)	(0.003)	(0.003)	(0.004)
Spinoff type 2 (β_{32})					-0.029***	-0.021***	-0.001	-0.003
					(0.003)	(0.002)	(0.002)	(0.003)
Firm type x Positive cluster growth:								
Positive cluster growth x New firm (β_4)		0.025***						
		(0.003)						
Positive cluster growth x Spinoff (β_4)				0.046***				
				(0.006)				
Positive cluster growth x Spinoff type 1 (β_4)						0.064***	0.030***	0.025**
						(0.009)	(0.008)	(0.012)
Positive cluster growth x Spinoff type 2 (β_4)						0.030***	0.021***	0.022**
						(0.007)	(0.006)	(0.011)
Controls for gender, age and education	no	no	no	no	no	no	yes	yes
Industry and Region fixed effects	no	no	no	no	no	no	yes	no
Industry x Region (= cluster) fixed effects	no	no	no	no	no	no	no	yes
Observations	188,044	188,044	51,767	51,767	51,767	51,767	51,554	51,554
R-squared	0.001	0.049	0.001	0.055	0.002	0.056	0.225	0.004

Notes: The dependent variable is the the share of employees with a tertiary education degree in the firm. The number of clusters is 1081, since some clusters do not contain any observations in 2010. See text for more details. Robust standard errors in parentheses. The R-squared in column 5 is computed on the de-meaned data. *** p<0.01, ** p<0.05, * p<0.1.

TABLE A4.3: Sales per Worker in New and Old Firms, Firm Level, 2010

	(1)	(2)	(3)	(4)	(5)	(6)	(7)	(8)
Constant (β_1)	13.410***	13.474***	13.038***	13.139***	13.038***	13.139***	13.763***	12.965***
	(0.002)	(0.003)	(0.005)	(0.006)	(0.005)	(0.006)	(0.153)	(0.024)
Positive cluster growth (β_2)		-0.189***		-0.222***		-0.222***	-0.027**	
		(0.005)		(0.010)		(0.010)	(0.012)	
Firm types:								
New firm (β_3)	-0.237***	-0.220***						
	(0.004)	(0.006)						
Spinoff (β_3)			0.231***	0.157***				
			(0.008)	(0.010)				
Spinoff type 1 (β_{31})					0.193***	0.120***	0.121***	0.114***
					(0.011)	(0.014)	(0.013)	(0.017)
Spinoff type 2 (β_{32})					0.256***	0.179***	0.158***	0.149***
					(0.009)	(0.011)	(0.010)	(0.014)
Firm type x Positive cluster growth:								
Positive cluster growth x New firm (β_4)		-0.008						
		(0.009)						
Positive cluster growth x Spinoff (β_4)				0.138***				
				(0.017)				
Positive cluster growth x Spinoff type 1 (β_4)						0.145***	0.073***	0.083***
						(0.023)	(0.021)	(0.029)
Positive cluster growth x Spinoff type 2 (β_4)						0.140***	0.017	0.034
						(0.021)	(0.018)	(0.030)
Controls for gender, age and education	no	no	no	no	no	no	yes	yes
Industry and Region fixed effects	no	no	no	no	no	no	yes	no
Industry x Region (= cluster) fixed effects	no	no	no	no	no	no	no	yes
Observations	178,152	178,152	49,182	49,182	49,182	49,182	48,999	48,999
R-squared	0.016	0.027	0.016	0.028	0.017	0.028	0.248	0.013

Notes: The dependent variable is the log of sales (revenue) per worker. The number of clusters is 1021, since some clusteres do not contain any observations in 2010. See text for more details. Robust standard errors in parentheses. The R-squared in column 5 is computed on the de-meaned data.
*** p<0.01, ** p<0.05, * p<0.1.

TABLE A4.4: Productivity in New and Old Firms, 2010

	(1)	(2)	(3)	(4)	(5)	(6)	(7)	(8)
Constant (β_1)	7.110***	7.029***	6.903***	6.805***	6.902***	6.805***	6.197***	6.434***
	(0.022)	(0.022)	(0.040)	(0.041)	(0.040)	(0.041)	(0.123)	(0.097)
Positive cluster growth (β_2)		0.062***		0.076***		0.076***	-0.014	
		(0.004)		(0.009)		(0.009)	(0.011)	
Firm types:								
New firm (β_3)	-0.041***	-0.066***						
	(0.004)	(0.004)						
Spinoff (β_3)			0.114***	0.096***				
			(0.007)	(0.008)				
Spinoff type 1 (β_{31})					0.115***	0.084***	0.076***	0.072***
					(0.010)	(0.011)	(0.011)	(0.012)
Spinoff type 2 (β_{32})					0.114***	0.103***	0.085***	0.076***
					(0.008)	(0.009)	(0.009)	(0.008)
Firm type x Positive cluster growth:								
Positive cluster growth x New firm (β_4)		0.062***						
		(0.008)						
Positive cluster growth x Spinoff (β_4)				0.080***				
				(0.015)				
Positive cluster growth x Spinoff type 1 (β_4)						0.106***	0.038*	0.046*
						(0.022)	(0.020)	(0.026)
Positive cluster growth x Spinoff type 2 (β_4)						0.062***	0.035**	0.055**
						(0.019)	(0.017)	(0.024)
log_kob_emp	0.396***	0.401***	0.338***	0.346***	0.338***	0.346***	0.343***	0.343***
	(0.002)	(0.002)	(0.003)	(0.003)	(0.003)	(0.003)	(0.004)	(0.017)
log_kap_emp	0.115***	0.114***	0.186***	0.184***	0.186***	0.184***	0.207***	0.207***
	(0.001)	(0.001)	(0.003)	(0.003)	(0.003)	(0.003)	(0.003)	(0.012)
log_emp	0.054***	0.053***	0.030***	0.030***	0.030***	0.030***	0.083***	0.082***
	(0.001)	(0.001)	(0.004)	(0.004)	(0.004)	(0.004)	(0.004)	(0.010)
Controls for gender, age and education	no	no	no	no	no	no	yes	yes
Industry and Region fixed effects	no	no	no	no	no	no	yes	no
Industry x Region (= cluster) fixed effects	no	no	no	no	no	no	no	yes
Observations	133,087	133,087	35,222	35,222	35,222	35,222	35,099	35,099
R-squared	0.528	0.530	0.480	0.484	0.480	0.484	0.577	0.474

Notes: The dependent variable is the log of sales (revenue) per worker in the firm. See text for more details. Robust standard errors in parentheses. The R-squared in column 5 is computed on the de-meaned data. The number of clusters is 975. *** $p<0.01$, ** $p<0.05$, * $p<0.1$.